Ridiculously Innovative

Ridiculously Innovative:

GENERATE AND APPLY MORE IDEAS FASTER TO GROW YOUR BUSINESS

Gary Covert

ISBN: 9781089524892

INTRODUCTION

M ost leaders will agree that raising the bar is critical to the current performance and future viability of their businesses. Many, however, don't do innovation as effectively as they could. Reasons include feeling that they are too busy, thinking it is too complicated, or wondering where to even start.

Leaders *are* busy, but they know conditions are changing. And they know they need to do something different. They know they can't just stay where they are.

This book is here to help leaders think about innovation differently—to view it as an essential skill that all parts of the organization can develop and a process in which many can participate. Innovation is critical to taking advantage of opportunities today and staying relevant tomorrow. In other words, we need to get in innovative shape now and stay in innovative shape for the future.

Many great companies started out as strong innovators, then faded as conditions changed. We have all seen the results of lapses in innovation over time. Sears started as an incredibly innovative company, selling everything under the sun through its catalogs. FTD, the flower delivery service, enjoyed great success by exploiting the power of the telegraph.

Toys "R" Us created and dominated a new market space in the form of big-box toy outlets. The shared downfall of these companies cannot be blithely dismissed as being due to troubles with "the internet." They had as much access to the internet as anyone. They also had the advantages of cash flow, brand recognition, and access to capital. Why then could they not make the turn? Why—when, in the past, they had been ridiculously innovative—did they lose their edge?

This book is perfect for leaders who want to better equip themselves to harness the creativity around them and apply it to grow their business more effectively. This book provides useful and practical tools for leaders to be much better innovators and to foster a better innovation culture. Plus, this book explains how to fill the gaps in leader capabilities that may be limiting the degree to which an organization is applying its creativity.

Many organizations do not rely on a central R&D function, but they still need to be able to harness the creativity of their people in a coherent and cohesive way. Even organizations that do have a very centralized R & D function will benefit from having leaders within the rest of the organization who are more adept at bringing their horsepower to bear on innovation initiatives.

The processes I am suggesting in this book don't need to replace continuous improvement committees or departments, but by putting the processes and responsibilities of these initiatives in the hands of leaders, those same initiatives will be even more impactful.

With this book, I want leaders to realize:

1. Yes, you can tap into people's creativity to improve your business.
2. Yes, you can innovate continuously.
3. Yes, you can improve the implementation of your ideas.

If the idea of better equipping yourself to stay relevant and elevate your organization to another level is attractive, read on, and let's get started.

CHAPTER ONE

The Urgency

The biggest mistake leaders can make is to act as if they can defer innovation. Organizations cannot afford to defer innovation any more than investors can afford to defer investments in their retirement. It is a rare individual who can time the market, and it is a rare organization that can successfully time innovation.

Most success is derived from *consistent* efforts, not sporadic efforts. The same can be said of physical fitness; those who stay consistent with a regimen of exercise and diet will see lasting results. The ones who yo-yo with their diet or only work out when they feel like it will not.

Conditions in the market are continuously changing. Leaders need to make sure their organizations are prepared for the inevitable threats and opportunities that change will bring. Leaders also need to make sure they don't get stuck on "Someday Island." Someday Island is a place full of excuses and wasted potential. Innovation is not reserved for some ideal future when things are less busy. If leaders don't take decisive action, the currents will inevitably pull them toward the rocks of Someday Island, and there they will sit, surrounded by an ocean of opportunity, unable to set sail.

The long list of companies that were innovative once but lost their edge includes:

- Kodak
- Nokia
- Xerox
- Blockbuster
- IBM
- JCPenney
- Blackberry
- Sears
- Radio Shack
- Motorola
- Borders
- Circuit City
- Toys "R" Us
- Tower Records

All these companies held strong market positions. All had advantages in their respective marketplaces, but all made some missteps or were slow to react to market changes. All these companies had smart, hardworking, well-intentioned people working for them, yet they weren't innovative enough to take the steps necessary to thrive.

But innovation isn't just about long-term survival. It's also about creating enormous short-term value, too. I have worked with many leaders to develop ideas that saved money or grew revenue in the short term. A physical fitness analogy works again here. Just like working out can have benefits for longevity, as well as short-term benefits like stress reduction and lower blood pressure, innovation can create short-term as well as long-term benefits. It's not just about surviving in the long term. It's also about thriving in the here and now.

But whether we are concerned about short-term effectiveness or long-term viability, the truth is that we can't stay put. Organizations need to consistent *and* proactively evolve.

CHAPTER TWO

Fine-tuning Your Good Idea Machine

An organization can either be a good idea machine or a bad idea machine. Good idea machines consistently generate quality ideas that are used to raise the performance bar. Bad idea machines might manage to produce a good idea every once in a while, but not frequently or consistently enough to make a substantial difference.

An idea machine has four components that work together like gears in an engine. These components are:

1. People giving input
2. Supervisors "screening in" ideas
3. Leaders selecting and supporting ideas
4. Doers driving execution

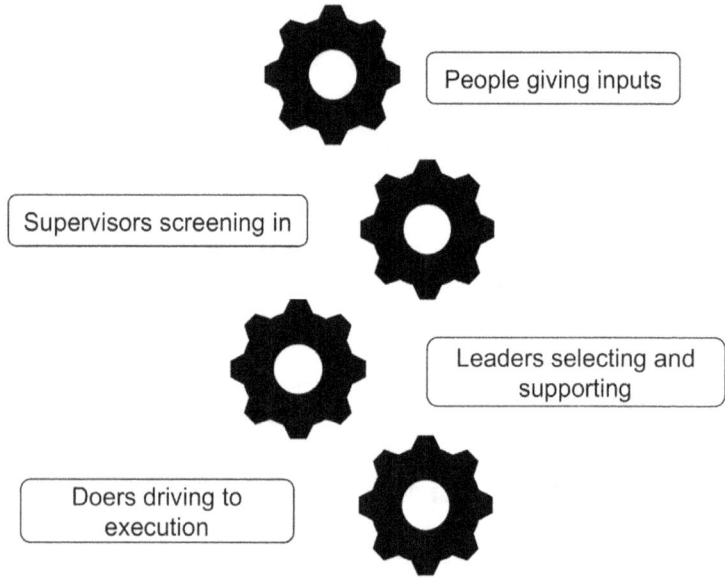

[FIGURE 1: COMPONENTS OF A GOOD IDEA MACHINE]

All these components must work together in order to produce ideas, turn them into opportunities, and see results. If any one part is missing or not in good working order, the result will be poor or sporadic innovation.

COMPONENT 1: PEOPLE GIVING INPUT

The first component is critical. Leaders have to encourage people to brainstorm new ways to improve the business, and they must be willing to share those ideas. Why don't people share more ideas? There are three possibilities.

1. They don't know that their leaders want their ideas. They may assume that the organization isn't interested in their input. (They may have good reasons for believing that.)
2. Their direct supervisors may be poor at handling new ideas. This is why the second part of the good idea machine is so important.
3. They may not know how to structure their ideas in a way that leaders can understand. I have worked with many front-line people to flesh out their ideas, and I've found that many believe that telling their supervisors about a good idea is enough, so they stop there.

People need to be appropriately prepared to share their ideas, and that requires clear indications from leadership that input is truly valued. It is also important to give some guidance to make sure that the insights given are of the highest possible quality. In the case of data input, there is the axiom of "garbage in, garbage out." The same applies to getting quality ideas in the pipeline.

The keys to getting quality ideas are:

• Be specific on areas

Be specific about the kinds of ideas where you would like to innovate. At any given time, the organization may have priorities like capital expenditure reduction, better customer service, operational efficiencies, or how to bring new hires up to speed faster. Let people know what the priorities are and what the current areas of interest are. While the door is always open to good ideas (whatever their area of improvement or potential impact may be), it is good to prime the pump and get people thinking in specific directions.

• Be specific about steps

Too often, when companies are asking for ideas, they are also asking for complete plans. Ideation and writing a plan should be considered distinct steps and should not be misconstrued. The first step is to simply get the idea out on the table.

• Be broad in participation

Ideas to improve an organization can come from anywhere, but many organizations limit their own potential by assuming that great ideas must come from the top or from a specific area like business development or R&D. With an appropriate process, quality ideas can be pulled from various units across an organization. Make sure all parts of the team understand that they are expected to be contributing their brainpower to raising the bar.

COMPONENT 2: SUPERVISORS "SCREENING IN" IDEAS

The second component of a good idea machine is leaders who can screen *in* good ideas as well as screen bad ones *out*. At the time of this writing, unemployment is at an all-time low. Companies are scrambling for talent and need to be much more flexible in order to get the talent they need. Many are being forced to alter their model of screening out poor candidates and are instead look for ways to screen strong ones in.

This concept is especially critical for leaders working with ideas that come from their teams. They need to be able to bring ideas in, help people improve them, and determine if they are of a viable quality and a high enough priority to be worthy of the investment of time and attention it will take to implement them.

What leaders don't want is to be on the extremes of open-mindedness and close-mindedness.

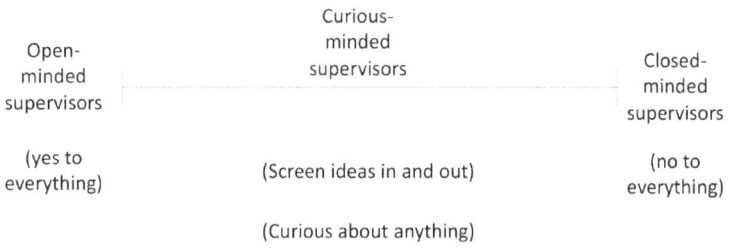

| Open-
minded
supervisors | Curious-
minded
supervisors | Closed-
minded
supervisors |

(yes to everything) (Screen ideas in and out) (no to everything)

(Curious about anything)

[FIGURE 2: OPEN-MINDED VS. CLOSED-MINDED]

On one extreme are those leaders who are so open-minded that they want to say yes to everything. They want to empower their people, and they feel they're getting in the way if they ask questions or say no. They want people to "go for it" and like to see themselves as supporting efforts rather than meddling in them or undercutting them. They often say things like, "I could only mess things up." What these leaders miss is that there is some benefit to having a structure.

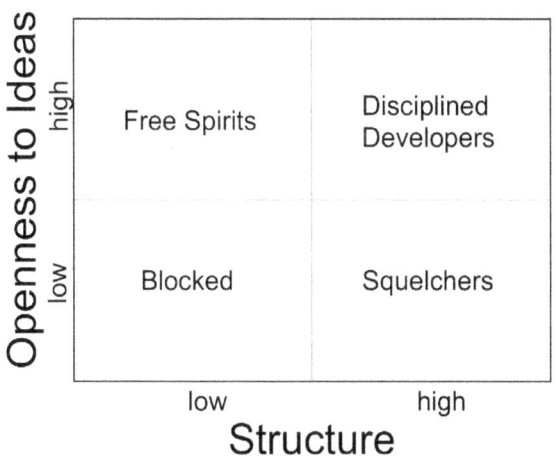

[FIGURE 3: OPEN TO IDEAS VS. STRUCTURE]

The downside of being unstructured and overly open is that new ideas may be poorly developed, not highly conducive with the priorities of the company, or ultimately unworkable.

On the other extreme, you have leaders who are, in effect, closed-minded. They squelch ideas. The stop the process prematurely. They are not very open, and they value control. Their strong point is that they can say "no" and minimize possible distractions. The downsides, meanwhile, are obvious: No new ideas will come from the team, innovators will become frustrated and stop innovating or leave, and engagement will be diminished.

The way a leader chooses to deal with new ideas has a huge impact. The worst example I have seen is a leader who literally shaped his fingers into machine guns and made the sound of bullets when shooting down ideas. He seemed to take particular pleasure in it. He was obviously an awful leader who, as a result, had very few ideas brought to him. This is an extreme example, but it illustrates the point that leaders need to be careful about how they react to people's ideas.

For many employees, it requires an act of courage just to bring an idea up. For some, their idea is their "baby." Immediately calling it ugly would obviously shut these people down. Of course, there are also lots of half-baked ideas out there. Not all will be beneficial or even practical. And not all will offer immediate value. That is why supervisors who can screen *in* are so vital.

Leaders need to avoid the extremes and be adept at screening ideas in to build coherent innovation. That means having the ability to discuss ideas with their direct reports and having both parties come together to reach a better understanding of the value, risk, and timeliness of the idea.

COMPONENT 3: LEADERS SELECTING AND SUPPORTING IDEAS

The third component of a good idea machine is leaders who can select and support specific ideas. Good ideas don't just turn into improvements automatically. It is essential to have leaders who can select the specific ideas that are the best, then work on these. Good ideas are as common as talented failures. True opportunities are more rare. There needs to be discipline and structure to manifest value.

At this point, the original idea is more than just an idea; it is now what I call an *investible opportunity*. At the point of selecting, leaders are nominating opportunities that are worthy of investment. The world is full of great ideas. What's rarer are ideas into which we should invest time and resources. An investible opportunity is an idea that is reliable enough that people want to invest their time and money in it, *and* in which they are willing to take some risk.

Good Idea	Investible Opportunity
Vague value	Common agreement on value and risk profile
Vague risk profile	Comprehensive description of critical issues
Low rigor on critical issues	High alignment with priorities
1 willing to sell	Many willing to buy

[TABLE 1 GOOD IDEA VERSUS INVESTIBLE OPPORTUNITY]

A leader knows they are doing a good job at screening in ideas when:

- There is a steady stream of ideas from the team and direct reports
- Some ideas can be graduated to the status of investible opportunities through dialog and debate
- Some ideas may be found to not be investible opportunities, and people still feel good about the process

Once ideas are screened in (or out, if they ultimately do not seem viable), they need to be put forward for approval. Every organization's approval processes will be different and may also change based on the scope of the proposal. Some proposals will be large in terms of impact or investment and will need formal approval from senior or executive leadership. Other opportunities may be smaller and may not need any approval beyond the manager. Whatever the case, at this stage, it needs to be clear whether what is being presented is an opportunity or a full-blown plan. An opportunity will have high rigor around risks, critical issues, alignment with priorities, costs, benefits, and likely level of disruption, but it does not need to have all the elements of a formal plan.

Leaders need to be rigorous when selecting ideas but also approach with the mindset of screening in. The review of an opportunity does not have to be a vote of "yes" or "no." The feedback may be, "yes, if you can show more benefits" or, "yes, if you can show how those risks are better mitigated."

My strong suggestion to leaders is to propose opportunities. Then, if there is sufficient interest, ask for a formal plan with timelines and other details. Many times, during the proposal process, senior leaders will raise valid questions about risks and opportunities that were not yet considered. These can be addressed and used to make a plan stronger, but you would hate for a person to pour a huge amount of effort into a formal plan only to have it simply shot down.

The other piece of this component is having leaders able to support ideas. This means leaders who are able to shield and nurture opportunities over time. In the desert, giant saguaros cacti start out small, living in the shelter of little bushes. These bushes act as protection for the saguaros until they can get their roots. Likewise, leaders need to nurture and support these ideas until they can stabilize and grow. Having a strong process of screening in ideas will also give leaders the confidence required when (inevitably) an idea needs to be defended or strongly advocated.

COMPONENT 4: DOERS DRIVING EXECUTION

The fourth component of a good idea machine is doers who can drive execution. The purpose of the process of innovation is to improve conditions for the organization—more revenue, more profits, new markets served, or new products offered. To do this, the organization needs to get these ideas implemented.

Leaders of organizations tell me that their most common area of concern is implementation. If people follow the steps of innovation (and do not skip straight from having an idea to "Go"), they can prevent some of the common issues that affect implementation, such as doing too many things at once, having initiatives working at cross-purposes, or not having appropriate input from other branches of the organization prior to launch. However, there is no getting around the fact that organizations need implementers to get new ideas started.

This can be tricky because the people required to conduct the implementation already have full-time jobs. They will need to balance attending to day-to-day tasks while they put new practices into place. That's why it is essential to include people, develop clarity on critical issues, and formulate robust plans.

Leaders need to equip a strong group of implementers in order to benefit from the ideas generated in an organization. Unfortunately, most organizations don't have a dedicated cadre of charge management professionals with nothing else to do except implement new projects. Even the organizations that do still need key people to act as implementers within the organization. At some point, people with other full-time responsibilities will need to be asked to take on new tasks to make sure the implementation works, which is why following a cohesive innovation process is critical.

GOOD AND BAD IDEA MACHINES

Remember, an organization can either be a good idea machine or a bad idea machine. Good idea machines have all four elements in place, working together. When that happens, an organization can turn the crank on ideas more effectively. They can produce more ideas faster and start to see traction from their efforts sooner.

Symptoms of a bad idea machine:
- Infrequent or inconsistent ideas generated
- People feeling disengaged because their ideas are "not heard"
- Ideas primarily coming from the same people or the same parts of the organization
- Poor or inconsistent implementation of ideas
- Low or poor awareness of what kinds of improvement initiatives the organization is interested in

Once leaders start to identify and understand the pieces of a good idea machine, they can begin to bolster and tune those areas to work more effectively and consistently.

EXERCISE

Rate each component of your organization on a scale of one to five (five being the best) for each aspect of a good idea machine.

1. People giving input
2. Supervisors "screening in" ideas
3. Leaders selecting and supporting ideas
4. Doers driving execution

Why did you score each component the way you did? What steps can you take to move up one level up in each category? If you scored one component as a five, what can you do to maintain the condition?

CHAPTER THREE

Create a Consistent Volume of Innovation

A key part of success in innovation is creating enough volume. Too many leaders think that innovation is only about breakthrough products. They ignore the more down-to-earth opportunities that might be right under their nose. There are likely plenty of ways to raise the bar that don't require a big R&D department or huge investments in capital. An innovation doesn't need to be some big, far-out development. As one of my clients puts it, "Not everything has to be the equivalent of an antigravity machine."

Leaders can create enormous value by increasing the volume of innovation initiatives. Once they have all four elements of a good idea machine in place, they should be able to work effectively on a wide array of initiatives. Some large. Some small. All consistently moving along multiple "S-curves" at the same time.

The S-curve is a common way to describe a specific innovation within a company. It refers to the level of performance that has been raised versus the level of effort. What leaders need to realize is that they can be working on multiple S-curves at any given time. They can be working on efforts that have shorter time horizons and smaller benefits right alongside much larger efforts with longer time horizons. An organization can capture an abundance of value by working multiple S-curves at the same time.

Using a baseball analogy, at any given time, an organization may be working on one or more of the following four types of innovations:

1. GAME-CHANGERS

These are completely new products, services, or business models that haven't been seen in the industry before. A game-changer requires the application of great effort and often takes years of dedicated investment. A game-changing innovation would put an organization far ahead of the competition or create a space where no competition yet exists.

2. HOME RUNS

Home-run innovations are those that make a company distinctly more competitive or efficient. A successful home run might boost create new revenue, dramatically improve the attractiveness of products and services, or widen the distinction between the company and its competition. Clients and competition would definitely notice the advance.

3. SCORING RUNS

Scoring runs are those innovations that produce incremental benefits for the company. The company and its clients would likely notice the improvement.

4. BASE-HITS

Base-hits are incremental improvements. The improvements would likely be noticed within the organization and serve as setups for larger future gains.

An organization can be working on big items that might result in a game-changing innovation or a home-run innovation while still scoring runs and racking up base hits. Leaders should be looking to make scoring runs every year and base hits every quarter while they work hard to find and execute on home runs and potential game-changers.

[Figure 4 Multiple S Curves]

The key point is to widen the view of innovation. Innovation is not just for big initiatives from R&D or the head office. Innovation should occur with continuous discipline. This is something that broad areas of the organization can participate in and from which we can see consistent growth and improvement, even while the very big breakthroughs are being pursued. Leaders should look for ways to attain value in big and small ways over time.

EXERCISE

What are some examples of each of the types of innovation (game-changers, home runs, scoring runs, and base hits) in your organization? How well has your organization done in terms of filling out its potential volume of innovation?

CHAPTER FOUR

Addressing Internal Barriers

C hange for the better is not easy. But sometimes, leaders make it even harder on themselves.

Innovation needs to have the right conditions in order to get off the ground, and there are certain barriers that occur inside our organizations that can obstruct our progress. Sometimes, we can be our own worst enemies. Let's look at some of the internal threats to innovation and what can we do about them.

There are many potential internal barriers to innovation, but three are stand-outs: an imbalance focus in terms of competition, self-protection, and lack of focus.

BARRIER 1: IMBALANCE OF FOCUS

Organizations can have an imbalance between where they put their focus (internal versus external) and their degree of competitiveness.

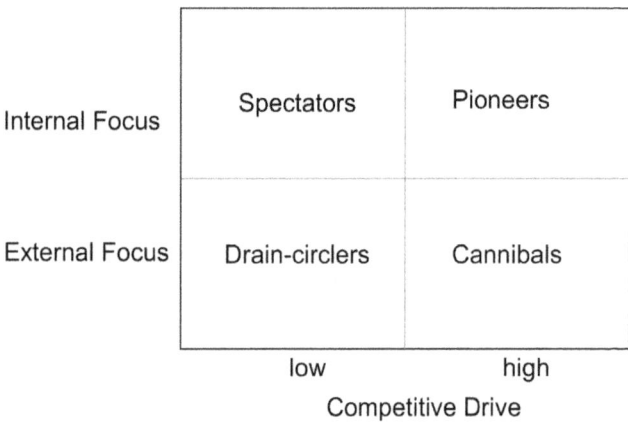

[FIGURE 5: FOCUS V. COMPETITION]

There are organizations that have such a problem with this that they could even be described as cannibalistic. They have a high degree of competitive drive, but it tends to be focused *internally* versus externally. Divisions compete against one another to the detriment of the larger good. These organizations do not innovate well because various groups cannot get out of their way to cooperate enough to make progress. Everyone's individual agenda comes first, and the overall effectiveness of the organization is lost.

Competition from within is what I call the *cannibalism zone*. A cannibalistic team or organization needs to redirect their energies in order to innovate. This is a malady that can only be cured through leadership.

On the opposite extreme from the cannibals are organizations that can be described as being in the *spectator zone*. Spectators are aware of what their customers need. They may also be aware of what their competitors are doing. However, they cannot seem to manifest their own competitiveness. Many nonprofit organizations have this issue. In this zone, an organization is focused on what the competition is doing but does not have sufficient focus to develop its own competitive spirit. These kinds of organizations are concerned with things like "the competitive benchmark" but do not put the appropriate energy into raising up their *own* game.

Leaders whose organization are in this zone either need to find people who will be either more competitive or very specific about raising their own internal benchmarks—and meeting them. Leaders need to make sure the competitive spirit *is* there and pointed in the right direction.

Some organizations may even be in the *drain-circling zone*. These organizations need to both raise their own competitiveness and get up to speed on what is happening in the world and with their customers.

Ideally, we want our organizations to be in the *pioneering zone*. Pioneers are always looking to the next horizon but also have a great drive to persevere and keep going. Companies in this zone have a solid focus on external issues *and* want to win. Great examples of companies currently in the pioneering zone include Apple, Nike, and Amazon. All are very aggressive companies, but they are also fanatically focused on their customers.

BARRIER 2: SELF-PROTECTION

The second barrier to effective innovation is self-protection. Any innovation initiative will require something that currently exists to change. And in any organization, anything that exists also has managers and departments responsible for maintaining it. Things that might change include processes, products, or business models. Leaders need to be sensitive to the fact that an innovation may impact who is doing what.

Most leaders and workers alike want to see their organization improve, but there may be resistance from people who want to preserve their old turf or just aren't sure how they will fit into the new scheme. This can potentially slow people down and divert precious energy.

BARRIER 3: LACK OF FOCUS

The third key barrier is lack of focus. In the first barrier (competition), I discussed internal focus versus external focus. Here, I am highlighting the *absence* of focus. For innovation efforts to be effective, they must be connected at the hip with strategy. Leaders cannot be chasing shiny objects that are not in alignment with the nature and direction of the company.

If the strategy is unclear and/or people are pulling in many different directions, truly valuable innovation is unlikely to come to fruition. Leaders need to be certain of the direction, and they must make sure they don't have so many things going on at once that they wear people out and dilute their efforts.

People need to know they are working on the few key things they *should* be working on instead one of the infinite number of things they *could* be working on. Leaders need to be discerning about initiatives and must ensure that they are in alignment with the strategic direction—not merely shiny objects pursued because they glittered at the right time.

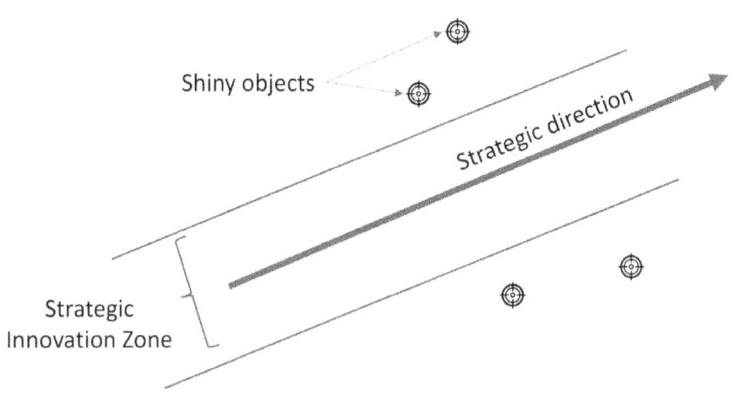

[FIGURE 6: STRATEGIC FOCUS]

There are many things that are outside a leader's control, but appropriate competition, possible reactions to the threats of charge, and degree of focus are all within a leader's discretion and must be taken into account if innovation efforts are to take root and thrive.

EXERCISE

How would you categorize your organization or team (spectators, cannibals, drain-circlers, or pioneers)? What needs to shift, and what needs to be maintained?

Creating Momentum

How do you boost momentum and get started driving innovation in your team or organization? First, leaders need to address four key factors: *what*, *who*, *why*, and *how*.

Get clear on *what* exactly you mean by "innovation." A clear definition will give a clear target to hit and get people on the same page.

Get clear on *why* innovation is important. Why is innovation worthy of our focus? Being able to convey the importance and urgency is needed to galvanize interest and buy-in.

Get clear on *how* this will be done. A leader will need to be able to map out the road ahead so people have a conceptual understanding of how this process will happen.

Get clear on *who* will be involved. Who should be involved? Clear articulation of who needs to be a part of the process is essential.

CLARITY ON *WHAT...*

What is innovation? *Ju-nin, to-iro* is a Japanese proverb meaning "ten people, ten different opinions." Ask ten people for their definition of innovation, and you will likely get ten (often muddled) answers.

The word "innovation" gets tossed around so casually, but there is little common understanding. My favorite definition is from Alan Weiss (co-author of *The Innovation Formula* with Michel Robert). Dr. Weiss defines innovation as "applied creativity." This means taking some idea that creates a new possibility and putting it into practice. Innovation, then, is not easy, but it *is* simple. We can use our creativity to come up with new options and find ways to apply them to improve the state or conditions of our organization.

Creativity without application, however, is simply dreaming. And application without creativity is mindless motion. We *need* and want both.

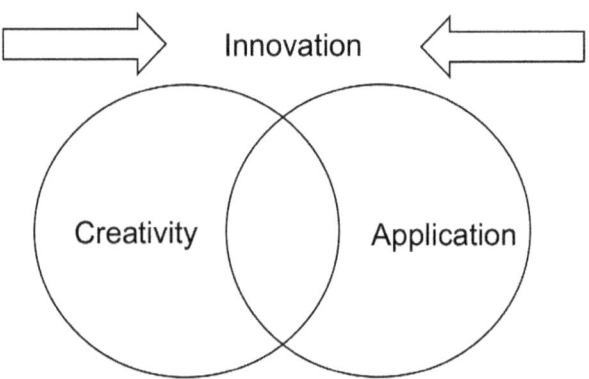

[FIGURE 7: CREATIVITY PLUS APPLICATION = INNOVATION]

So, what is the opposite of innovation? *Fixing*.

Fixing (or problem-solving) is an incredibly valuable activity. It gets things back to where they should be. Fixing a leaky canoe prevents it from sinking and makes it a good canoe again. But adding a sail to a canoe makes it better than it ever was. With a sail, it is not just a good canoe; it is something decidedly superior and different.

Leaders need to be excellent problem-solvers. Many are. Organizations have many processes for root cause analysis that systematize the process of fixing things. What they don't have are ways to systemize innovation. The result is organizations that are good at plugging the holes but haphazard about considering new ways to sail faster or farther.

Demystifying what exactly innovation is goes a long way toward helping people learn what they need to do. It helps them to see that they, too, can be in the innovation business. Anyone can participate on the creativity side, on the application side, or, very likely, on both.

Where some people get tripped up is when they think that innovation is exclusively a moonshot—a big gamble—or a word reserved for technological advances. Some of the most visible innovations did come from major breakthroughs in technology (the plane, the lightbulb, nuclear power, etc.), but less conspicuous innovations are made all the time that are nevertheless very valuable and don't require an Einstein or an Edison. For example:

- Apple's Genius Bar: a shift to a high-touch, high-aesthetic, one-on-one experience instead of a cold, arm's-length call center model
- Term life insurance instead of whole life
- Having customers use kiosks to input their own food orders instead of having a worker do it

- New categories of convenience services like mobile pet grooming (even mobile pet exercising on treadmills), mobile workout services, mobile food trucks, and people who will come and pick up pet waste in yards

I have coached many leaders on how to bring out their ideas so that senior leadership could get behind them. Many of these ideas did not require new capital investments or the hiring of new people. Many companies can make changes to processes, spend time in new pursuits, or rationalize who does what to create cost savings and raise new revenue sources. The key is not to limit innovative thinking or dismiss the value of shifts that aren't completely new creations.

Many things created by entrepreneurs are simple reorganizations of activities, processes, and target markets. I have seen leaders create new opportunities nearly out of thin air. It starts with giving up the limiting belief that innovation is for another time, another place, or another person.

CLARITY ON *WHY...*

The next phase in creating momentum is to get clear on the urgency of why innovation is important. Leaders ought to know the importance of innovation, but how well is that importance conveyed across the organization? People may hear "innovation is important." They may even see the word included in a list of corporate values. But do they really have a sense of urgency? Do they see it in the actions of their leaders? Leaders must realize that they cannot defer innovation. Does the rest of the organization know that as well?

Key points to convey urgency:

Sell yourself first. In order to convince anyone of anything, we must first convince ourselves. What do you think are some of the risks that might occur if your team does not continue to raise the bar? What are some opportunities you would hate to see lost?

Create some compelling examples. What are some cautionary tales in your company or industry? The business section is rife with relatable examples of organizations that have been left by the wayside (see Chapter One for a full list). What are some that resonate with you? Are there examples of companies who fell by the wayside in your industry? Are there examples of great companies who have taken the lion's share of business or have a reputation for staying out in front? Does your organization have a success tale? Or a cautionary tale?

Communicate urgency in big doses and small doses. Once you have convinced yourself and have some compelling examples, make a plan to communicate. Big doses come during large company functions like leadership retreats or town halls. Communicate the urgency in these large-audience platforms. Also communicate in smaller doses, like in small team meetings and one-on-ones. There needs to be sufficient volume and variety so that the organization realizes something is different and new.

CLARITY ON *HOW*...

The next step is to address the *how*. Asking people if they want to win will always elicit a "yes," but people also want some concept of how that will happen. They need to see some connection between the future you are offering them and where they are now. Unfortunately, "innovation" is a word thrown around so casually that it has become meaningless to many people. They may like the concept but be skeptical about the practicality.

At this point, you simply want to share the basic outline of the steps of innovation.

- Ideas will be generated
- Ideas will be screened in/out
- Ideas will be developed
- Plans will be made
- Opportunities will be implemented

How these steps are followed will be different for every organization. Some leaders may want to follow this process one-on-one with their team. Other leaders may want to do this more formally in a workshop format with an experienced facilitator. With a clear understanding of the process, people will know what the expectations are and how they can contribute.

CLARITY ON *WHO*...

The next consideration is *who* will be involved in innovation efforts. I would suggest that leaders consider going both deep and broad. "Deep" means going down through the organization and moving toward the front line to get ideas. I don't mean more "listening" sessions where people from corporate go and listen to people's reactions to initiatives. I mean going deep as a source of ideas to execute.

Traditional versus Inclusive Innovation

Traditional	Inclusive
• Innovation made in isolation • Input gathered reactively • Input used for adjustment of existing plans	• Innovation done broadly and deeply • Insights uncovered proactively • Input used to collaboratively create opportunities

[FIGURE 8 TRADITIONAL VERSUS INCLUSIVE INNOVATION]

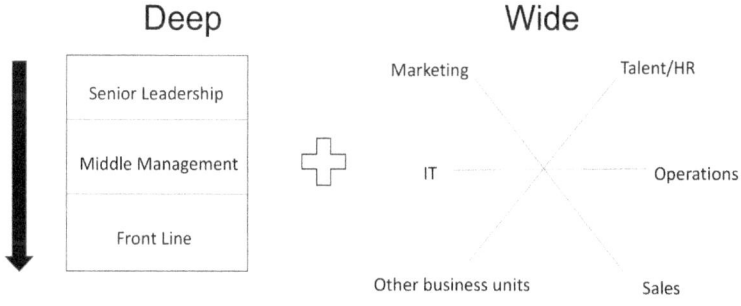

[FIGURE 9 INNOVATION SOURCES: DEEP AND WIDE]

A leader will also want to consider going wide. I was facilitating a session with a group of executives when the senior HR leader said her biggest revelation was that she had a fundamental role to play in the process of innovation. This is obvious but often ignored. The more people from across an organization are brought in—and brought in at the idea stage—the more high-quality ideas will be generated, and the more buy-in will occur.

Any innovation in the organization will require various parts to work together. Leaders can see great benefits when they encourage teams to work together from the beginning.

There are four prime reasons for going deep and wide.

1. Increased quality of ideas
2. Reduced risk from unintended consequences
3. Improved buy-in
4. Less disruption in the implementation stage

EXERCISE

What is the urgency for innovation in your organization? Who needs to hear that, and how will you convey it?

Why Implementation Efforts Fail and What to Do about It

"A revolution is an idea that has found its bayonets."
—Napoleon Bonaparte

Leaders are often frustrated because there are plenty of ideas to improve the business but cannot get them across the finish line in a timely manner. Initiatives are frequently started with great enthusiasm only to soon peter out.

Many people want to get in shape. They buy the Bowflex or the gym membership, and a year later, nothing has changed. The same problem occurs in organizations. When nothing has changed, leaders don't like the fact that the results were not achieved, but they also hate all the wasted effort.

There are *general* reasons that any effort to improve will fail. There are also *specific* reasons that are unique to failed attempts to innovate. We will look at the general reasons first. There are five possible reasons that good intentions don't work, and these five reasons apply to any improvement we are trying to make, whether in the gym or as a leader.

GENERAL REASON 1: POOR PLAN QUALITY

Your plans need to provide the concrete steps to get to your goal. By definition, some plans are not, in fact, plans. "Going to the gym" is not a plan. "Eating better" is not a plan. But developing specific regimens (based on science, not fads) for nutrition and exercise is a plan. If a person (or team) does not have the expertise to create the plan, then expert help is required.

GENERAL REASON 2: POOR SUPPORT NETWORK

A person who wants to run a marathon or lose weight needs the support of people around them to succeed. They need a team to encourage them and keep them accountable. In an organization, implementation will fall apart if key leaders and teams are not actively working to provide encouragement.

GENERAL REASON 3: LOW LEVEL OF CONVICTION

Conviction is the strong belief in something. The people doing the work and those supporting the effort need to truly believe that the activity is worthy of sacrifice.

GENERAL REASON 4: POOR DISCIPLINE

To achieve results, we need to stay consistent. We need to diligently stay on target, keep our commitments, and make timely adjustments. We must stay consistent and work through the process.

GENERAL REASON 5: LOW LEVEL OF EFFORT

We are unlikely to make progress on anything worthwhile without breaking a sweat. Making something better while we are meeting other commitments at work takes real effort, and we should not kid ourselves about that.

Making any improvement requires 100 percent honesty about each of the five general factors listed above. In addition to the five general reasons, there are also five specific factors that can derail innovation efforts.

SPECIFIC REASON 1: LACK OF GOOD PEOPLE WITH THE BANDWIDTH TO CHAMPION THE EFFORT

Every innovation effort needs a champion to help push it through. The ideal champion will be knowledgeable about the details of the innovation and have the skills to rally people, focus attention, and navigate any organizational hurdles. But this person also must have the bandwidth to handle it; if they have too much on their plate, the initiative will not get the attention it deserves. If the initiative is championed by someone without the proper skills, that can be just as bad as having no champion at all.

SPECIFIC REASON 2: POOR INNOVATION PROCESS CONTROL

Innovation efforts should follow a coherent process. There are specific stages to follow, and people need to know what those stages are and how effectively each one was completed. Too often, organizations will try to skip steps and jump directly from an idea to "make it so." Skipping steps leaves crucial pieces of the puzzle covered—until people start to implement.

SPECIFIC REASON 3: MISALIGNMENT OF INCENTIVES

Incentives need to *support* the change, not undermine it. Leadership cannot expect people to change their behaviors while remaining calibrated to old behaviors. For example, a call center agent cannot be expected to spend more time exploring cross-selling opportunities with customers while also being rewarded for keeping calls as short as possible. Incentives must also be aligned across an organization. For example, an organization cannot expect sales growth of newly developed products if the sales department is equally recognized for the sale of *any* product.

SPECIFIC REASON 4: LACK OF RECOGNITION OF DISRUPTION AND MITIGATION EFFORTS

Innovation will change things, and it is likely that efficiencies will suffer anytime a new idea is tried. Trouble occurs when the potential for disruption is downplayed or not given appropriate analysis. Disruptions are not the problem. Rather, the problem is not anticipating disruptions and neglecting to develop plans to reduce the impact. This is particularly prevalent when innovation initiatives are just tossed over the fence from one group to another or developed in isolation with zero input from the groups that will be asked to implement them.

SPECIFIC REASON 5: TOO MANY SIMULTANEOUS "PRIORITIES"

People have infinite creativity but finite energy. We need to realize that an organization can only execute on so much at a given time. There may be lots of good things an organization *could* do, but there is likely a much smaller number of high-value things that they *ought to* do.

Based on the above issues, here are key actions to take to ensure great implementation of your innovation efforts.

Get control of the basics. Any improvement initiative needs a quality plan, a great support network, shared conviction of the need for innovation, discipline to see it through, and sufficient focused effort.

Have great champions that actually have the bandwidth to execute. Don't make the mistake of settling for the wrong champion just because they are available, and don't bury your top people under too much at once.

Make sure incentives are aligned with the desired future state, not tied to the current state. People need to be incentivized for what you want them to do, not what they are currently doing.

Follow a defined process that can take your idea to implementation. Don't attempt to wing it. In his talks and workshops on the subject of innovation, Alan Weiss highlights five distinct steps in the process: Ideation, Screening, Development, Planning, and Implementation. Jumping the gun and moving through these stages haphazardly will seed problems that will sprout like weeds in the implementation stage.

Be rigorous about unearthing potential disruptions in advance. Seek to minimize and mitigate. If the disruption risks are too high, that is a red flag that the effort needs to be reconsidered.

Be discriminating about priorities. Don't bite off more than the organization can chew at a given time.

EXERCISE

On a scale of one to five (five besting the best), how well does your organization execute on initiatives? If it's not as good as you would like, what do you think are some of the reasons?

CHAPTER SIX

Maintaining Innovation: How to Keep it a Priority

I t is critical to maintain innovation efforts once they're started. Maintaining consistency of effort is the only way to get results. Plus, innovation consistency tells the organization a lot about their leaders. It tells them that their leaders can walk the talk and that they are serious about raising the bar over time.

Benefitting from innovation efforts requires consistency. Consistent effort over time trumps sporadic, feverish efforts. Making things better requires real effort and energy, but it takes time to see the results.

A farmer displays a "patient busyness" as he tends his crops; he stays patient, but he also stays busy. The planting is just part of it. The soil requires preparation. The land requires irrigation. Weeds need to be pulled. Likewise, innovation demands careful attention over time. Things won't just sprout overnight. Innovation is not an event. It is a process.

So, why don't organizations keep up their innovation efforts?

They get busy with other things. The leadership and the team become focused on another issue or priority. Maybe there's a big client project that's due. Maybe there was a customer audit. Maybe there were unfavorable reports from outside financial analysts. There's always something urgent bubbling up, and it can overshadow important processes.

They get overwhelmed with too many things. The sheer volume of tasks and activities (even if they are small individually) leaches away vital energy and focus.

They get burned by a failure. Sometimes, things don't work. Sometimes, the effort makes things worse or doesn't pan out. Having a good process will help avoid this, but there is no guarantee that things won't go south. People need to know it's okay to make mistakes or have a failure.

They get discouraged when they don't see results right away. It takes time to see results. The Wright brothers took decades to work out each key principle of flight. But people often give up on the process when they don't see *immediate* results. Unfortunately, that's not a realistic expectation.

They don't consider it a priority anymore. An organization needs to be aware that efforts to raise the bar are still on the table and remain a high priority for the organization. Unfortunately, many people in organizations have witnessed "major plans" become nothing but faddish flavor-of-the-month initiatives that just seem to quietly fade away after a big splash. They need to know that these efforts are valued and that the eyes of the leadership are still on the process.

People move or change. It's a fact of modern organizational life that people will change jobs. New leaders come in. When this happens, priorities can change, or skills can be lost. Innovation is a habit and a process that needs senior-level support. The details may shift, but the direction for improvement (upward) needs to stay a constant.

THE FOUR KEYS TO MAINTAINING INNOVATION MOMENTUM

In addition to addressing the common reasons that innovation efforts lose their momentum, there are four keys to maintaining innovation momentum.

Make *manifesting innovation* part of the culture. Many companies use the word "innovation." Far fewer companies manifest innovation on a regular basis. The key is to not relegate "innovation" to the status of a corporate platitude—just one of several statements on a list of corporate values. People need to see innovation as a real process with tangible outcomes. The more people can see it (and better yet, participate in it), the better. This means seeing leaders effectively interacting with people and their ideas (like the skillful use of "screening in" ideas versus blunt screening out, highlighted earlier in this book). It means making innovations visible to the organization so that people can see effort and progress. It means having a culture where people can tell by the behaviors of leaders and supervisors that the company encourages prudent risk-taking and a healthy impatience with the status quo.

Go broad with skill. Make sure that people from across the organization are versed in the fundamentals of innovation. All leaders are expected to have strong communication skills. Why not innovation skills? The more people have the knowledge, the more opportunities the organization will be able to capture. This adds capacity across the organization and keeps those muscles strong even with the inevitable changes in personnel.

Reward participation in the process, **not just outcomes.** It takes time to improve, and sometimes, an initiative simply doesn't come to fruition despite everyone's best efforts. People need to be encouraged to keep at the process. The more consistent people are, the more skillful they will become, and the more likely their efforts will actually bear fruit in the future.

Formalize innovation efforts in the performance review process. As Peter Drucker observed, what gets measured gets managed. Employees need to know that innovation is at the front of their leaders' minds. Including innovation in the formal review process will help maintain some discipline and make the intent overt. Where it makes sense (and it will likely make sense for most managers and all senior leaders) ask, "In what ways are you helping to elevate performance standards in the organization?"

CHAPTER SEVEN

Developing, Retaining, and Attracting Innovation Rainmakers

While everyone in an organization can play a role in innovation, there are people who will likely be better at it than others. It may be because they are especially creative or because they are very entrepreneurial. It may be because they have a unique perspective that helps them see opportunities that others do not. I call these highly innovative people "innovation rainmakers" because of their oversized impact when it comes to the generation of new ideas. It is crucial that leaders do their best to support those who demonstrate this aptitude.

I was fortunate to have one of these rainmakers on my team when I was in a sales and marketing role. Marty was a chemist with the mind of a true salesperson. He brought many ideas to my attention. One idea still makes millions of dollars a year for our old company even a decade later.

I would never have had a clue that we could help our customers in new ways if he hadn't acted and come forward with the idea.

I come across many of these rainmakers as I work with clients. Not all of them are in top leadership positions. One rainmaker I met was in a supervisor position and had many great ideas (one of which, I helped him turn into an investible opportunity that he presented to senior leadership). His perspectives were worth enormous cost savings for his company.

Leaders need to be sensitive to the possibility that they have rainmakers within their organization. They aren't always the most vocal people in the room, and they're not always the most articulate. They may be the quiet thinkers—the contemplators. It is the leader's job to find these people and make sure they are developed and supported in the best way.

HOW DO YOU KNOW A POTENTIAL RAINMAKER WHEN YOU SEE ONE?

- They regularly make suggestions (or have suggestions when asked)
- They can see the bigger picture
- They have a healthy impatience with the status quo
- They are highly entrepreneurial
- They may surprise you with a great idea
- They can give examples of raising the bar at a past employer

It is a leader's job to be aware of innovation strength on their team and to do their best to develop it and make sure it stays. Below are some key actions:

Develop the skill further. Make sure they are not only good at ideation. Help them to be great at developing their ideas into investible opportunities, and make that part of their formal development plan.

Ask them to champion a project. This will give them the practical experience of moving an idea through an organization. Keep the project scope in relation to their maturity and experience.

Discuss innovation opportunities regularly. Let them know that you see them as someone with a useful perspective. Talk about opportunities to raise the bar in one-on-ones and other meetings.

Expand their exposure broadly across the organization. Find ways for them to meet other business or service units. Get them on committees. Have them sit in on meetings they may not otherwise have the opportunity to be in.

Rearrange their work to allow for some innovation bandwidth. A *Dilbert* cartoon made the sadly funny commentary that high performers frequently gather work until they are overloaded and become as mediocre as everyone else. Do your best to arrange work so that potential rainmakers have the opportunity to work on new things and see them through to fruition.

Make sure their manager values those skills and can help develop them. Managers play a huge role in our enjoyment at work. If a highly innovative person is working for a manager who either can't or won't support it, either rethink that manager or get the innovative person into a different situation that will work for them. Otherwise, that manager may be the principal reason the person decides to leave.

The truth is, highly innovative people need to express their innovative tendencies. I frequently quote Dr. Dan Harrison's research that people who enjoy their work 75 percent or more of the time are three times more likely to be successful at it. The concept applies here, too. Innovative people will thrive when they can innovate. If they cannot express their strengths, one of two things will happen:

1. They will *stay*, and their engagement will suffer.
2. They will *leave*, and the benefit could go to another company (and that may be your competition).

While I believe anyone can boost their innovation abilities, there are some people who clearly have more aptitude for it. When you see it, do your best to foster and keep it.

ON ATTRACTING INNOVATION TALENT

The best way to attract innovation talent is to be the sort of place that fosters innovation. This has to be more than a recruitment ploy. What I'm talking about is *attraction gravity*.

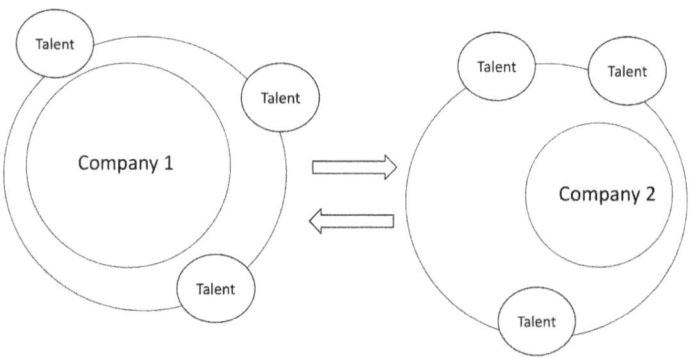

[FIGURE 10 ATTRACTION GRAVITY]

Companies that really have a culture of innovation will attract like-minded people. Your team will tell people that your organization is a great place to work because ideas are encouraged and developed. The stories that are written about your company will highlight new and valuable ways to do things. Your hiring managers will be able to point to specific examples of improvement and do so with pride and excitement.

All of these factors are irresistible to people who really want to improve things and have the fortitude and intellectual horsepower to see it to fruition. As an attraction strategy, a culture of innovation attracts better candidates than those who are attracted to a stocked pantry, ping-pong tables, and beanbag chairs in a decompression room with posters of the Dalai Lama.

EXERCISE

Who on your team has an aptitude for innovation? What can you do to support them?

IN CONCLUSION

I hope you found this brief book useful. Innovation is a critical activity. It raises the bar on performance today. It helps keep a company relevant for tomorrow. Innovative companies are fun places to be, and they attract the very best talent. It is not as mysterious a process as people may think.

We can see the impact of innovation in the most successful and most admired companies. The truth is, many other companies can innovate even more effectively, and with some basic skills and discipline, leaders can play a major role.

My thanks to the many leaders and organizations I have had the pleasure to work with. They continue to impress me with their hard work and dedication to making their companies more effective every day.

If you would like more information about how to implement innovation more effectively in your organization, please contact me to schedule a discussion.

Gary Covert

Gary Covert Consulting

www.garycovertconsulting.com

PO Box 51732

Phoenix, Arizona 85076

Phone: 480-720-9551

Email: gary@garycovertconsulting.com

THE RIDICULOUSLY INNOVATIVE MANIFESTO

Below are ten key points that will drive more effective innovation in your organization.

1. PARADIGMS SHIFTED ARE AS VALUABLE AS PARADIGMS BROKEN.

Not every improvement in your organization needs to be some big dramatic event. While technology grabs headlines for cool new products or services like foldable phones or using proton accelerators to smash cancer cells, more prosaic improvements count, too.

2. INNOVATION ON THE INSIDE REQUIRES COMPETITION ON THE OUTSIDE.

Raising the bar can threaten existing processes, existing technology, and even existing business models. And anything that is existing has managers, leaders, and teams that take care of these things. Senior leaders need to take care that smaller interests don't supplant the larger future gains that can come from new innovations.

3. IN MANY ORGANIZATIONS, INNOVATION FROM THE FRONT LINE IS FOUR TIMES MORE VALUABLE THAN INNOVATION FROM THE MOTHERSHIP.

For the many organizations that are less dependent on centralized R&D, the front line is a rich and often overlooked source of innovation. Plus, ideas from the front line can be 100 percent more practical and have 100 percent more buy-in, tend to be 100 percent less disruptive, and come with 100 percent less risk. Coherently bringing these ideas to light and efficiently implementing them can be an exceedingly beneficial approach.

4. INNOVATION IS IN EVERYONE'S JOB DESCRIPTION AND IS SOME-THING YOU *ASK* OF THE ORGANIZATION, NOT IMPOSE.

Every part of your organization can reset and improve its standards of performance. Just like every leader is expected to deliver results in their department or develop their people, we can and should expect people at every level to raise the bar and not just fix problems.

5. THE FASTEST WAY TO GROW YOUR BUSINESS IS DUMPING THE BOTTOM 10 PERCENT OF IDEAS AND ELEVATING THE TOP 10 PERCENT. SMART LEADERS "GO NEUTRON" ON THE WORST AND NURTURE THE BEST.

Jack Welch, former CEO of GE, was once known as "Neutron Jack." He was known to "go neutron" on people or business units he felt were not performing. Leaders today need to be equally rigorous about supporting good ideas and dumping bad ones. The degree to which leaders can accelerate the success of great ideas and minimize the impact of bad ideas is the real predictor of sustainable success.

6. GREAT INNOVATORS (LIKE RAINMAKERS) TEND TO LIKE THEIR OWN WEATHER. THE LEADER'S PRIME JOB IS TO MAKE SURE THAT THE ORGANIZATION ISN'T HANDING OUT UMBRELLAS AND SHOWING THEM THE DOOR.

Be wary that layers of management are not snuffing out great ideas or inducing people to express their creativity elsewhere.

7. INNOVATION IS NOT A LINEAR ASCENT; IT IS A SWITCHBACK.

Innovation is not always a straight, predictable path to the top. Be prepared for a consistent climb, sometimes out of sight of the summit, when all that can be seen is the hard work of the next task.

8. COMPLEXITY IS THE ENEMY OF INNOVATION. KILLING TWO BIRDS WITH ONE STONE DOES NOT REQUIRE A ROCK QUARRY.

Change for the better does not require grandiose plans or elaborate approaches. Keeping things simple and focused can create enormous value quickly.

9. THE NUMBER ONE CAUSE OF POOR INNOVATION IS SELF-AMPUTATION OF CREATIVITY. THE SECOND CAUSE IS POOR IMPLEMENTATION, WHICH IS TO SAY, SHOOTING YOURSELF IN THE FOOT.

People do themselves and others no service by denying their abilities or rejecting a role in developing ideas to improve the organization. Once ideas come to the surface, organizations must work diligently to apply them and actually derive the benefit.

10. ORGANIZATIONS SAYING THEY WILL INNOVATE WHEN THEY HAVE THE MONEY OR THE TIME IS THE SAME AS SAYING, "I'LL BREATHE AFTER I CATCH MY BREATH."

Businesses don't *do* innovation; innovation *is* business. Innovation is not some activity for a distant, ideal future. Raising the bar and finding ways to do things faster, better, or cheaper is the essence of business and is an activity for the here and now.